California Natural History Guides: 1

INTRODUCTION TO THE

NATURAL HISTORY

OF THE

SAN FRANCISCO BAY REGION

BY

ARTHUR C. SMITH

DRAWINGS BY GENE M. CHRISTMAN

UNIVERSITY OF CALIFORNIA PRESS

BERKELEY, LOS ANGELES, LONDON

UNIVERSITY OF CALIFORNIA PRESS

BERKELEY AND LOS ANGELES, CALIFORNIA

UNIVERSITY OF CALIFORNIA PRESS, LTD.

LONDON, ENGLAND

© 1959 BY

THE REGENTS OF THE UNIVERSITY OF CALIFORNIA

FOURTH PRINTING, 1971

ISBN: 0-520-01185-6

LIBRARY OF CONGRESS CATALOG CARD NUMBER: 59-6051

PRINTED IN THE UNITED STATES OF AMERICA

DESIGN BY JOHN B. GOETZ

CONTENTS

ILLUSTRATIONS ON COVER
   Ceanothus Silk Moth (*Hyalophora euryalus*)
   Fly Agaric (*Amanita muscaria*)
   Mountain Lilac (*Ceanothus thyrsiflorus*)
   American Avocet (*Recurvirostra americana*)

INTRODUCTION

Most of us are interested in the world around us. We wish that we knew the name of the beautiful bird that sings on the back fence every morning; we wonder what kind of a shell it was that we picked up at the beach last Sunday; or perhaps we would like to know if that small but ferocious-looking creature we found under a rock in the back yard is really as dangerous as it looks. All too often it is just too much trouble to find the answer, and we soon forget all about it.

This series of California Natural History Guides will help you find the answers to these and many other questions about the natural history of the back yards and vacant lots of our towns and cities; the mountains, valleys, ponds, streams, deserts and beaches of California.

You may find that some phase of nature study will provide just the added interest you have been seeking to make life more enjoyable. If you are a hunter or fisherman, you may want to learn more of the non-game animals that you see on your trips afield. If you are a teacher, youth leader, or student, you may wish to increase your store of facts about plants and animals around school, camp, or home. If you are a member of a youth organization, you may want help in qualifying for merit badges or other awards in nature subjects. If you have recently moved to this area, you may find the plants and animals so different from those you have known before that you are uncertain of your identifications. This series of guides will help you to identify the common plants and animals of this region.

Whether you are eight or eighty, you will find life more enjoyable if you become familiar with nature in the bay region. Studying and observing nature can be a highly satisfying yet economical year-around recreation for the entire family. Spring, summer, fall, and winter your family car can take you (with your California Natural History Guide in hand) to beaches, mountains, fields, and marshes where you can become acquainted with the birds, butterflies, shells, rocks and minerals, trees, flowers or other interesting subjects of your choice.

At first you will be content to learn their names. Later you will want to know, for example, where the birds nest, where to look for cocoons and chrysalids, or how to identify and preserve animal tracks. If you make careful observations and keep accurate notes, you may find that you can make worthwhile contributions to science, for the habits and the details in the life histories of many of our bay region animals are still unknown.

In this, the first volume of the series, there is a general introduction to the San Francisco Bay region —its physical features, climate, and seasons. This is followed by discussions of the characteristics of living things, common and scientific names of plants and animals, and the interrelationships in the world of nature. Special sections describe the biotic communities where plants and animals are found and suggest interesting field trips you can take in the bay region. Various nature activities are discussed, and organizations concerned with nature in the bay region are listed.

THE SAN FRANCISCO BAY REGION

PHYSICAL DESCRIPTION

In the California Natural History Guides the bay region is arbitrarily designated as the nine counties bordering San Francisco Bay plus Santa Cruz County.

Although the entire bay is generally called San Francisco Bay, the north part is known as San Pablo Bay, and its narrow easterly extension beyond Carquinez Strait as Suisun Bay.

The bay opens to the Pacific Ocean through the Golden Gate; covers a total area of some 900 square miles extending from Treasure Island approximately 30 miles to the southeast and 20 miles to the north; and reaches eastward from San Pablo Bay some 30 miles through Carquinez Strait along the drowned river valley of the Sacramento–San Joaquin rivers.

The bay varies from 3 to 13 miles in width (narrowing to half a mile at Carquinez Strait) with the main channel from 20 to 60 feet deep south of the Bay Bridge; from 30 to 130 feet deep between Treasure Island and Angel Island; from 220 to 357 feet deep beneath Golden Gate Bridge; varying from 20 to 54 feet from Treasure Island to San Pablo Strait; and with a maximum channel depth of 34 feet in San Pablo Bay (most of which is less than 10 feet deep). Carquinez Strait varies in depth from 94 feet at Carquinez Bridge to 38 feet at Martinez Yacht Harbor.

A number of small islands rise in the bay, mostly in the area bounded by the three major bridges.

The San Francisco and Marin peninsulas enclose the bay from the west, with Mount Tamalpais (2,604 ft.) dominating the Marin Peninsula, and the Montara and northern extension of the Santa Cruz Mountains

SAN FRANCISCO BAY REGION

rising back of the San Francisco Peninsula cities.

To the south of the bay lies the Santa Clara Valley, with the Santa Cruz Mountains on the west and the Mount Hamilton Range (a part of the Diablo Range) on the east. Mount Hamilton (4,209 ft.) dominates the eastern mountains. Loma Prieta (3,798 ft.) and Black Mountain (2,810 ft.) are two of the most prominent peaks seen west of the valley.

North of the bay a series of valleys and ridges parallels the coastline, with Mount St. Helena (4,344 ft.) rising at the head of the Napa Valley.

In Sonoma County north of Russian River a part of the eroded Mendocino Plateau enters our area.

The Berkeley Hills rise behind the East Bay cities, with paralleling ridges to the south and east. The Diablo Range extends from Mount Diablo (3,849 ft.) in Contra Costa County to just south of Pacheco Pass in Santa Clara County.

A part of the Great Central Valley enters the bay region in eastern Contra Costa and Solano counties.

There are no natural fresh-water lakes of any size in the area, but there are many reservoirs in the hills and mountains encircling the valleys. Most bay region streams are intermittent (dry for part of the year). Among the permanent streams are the San Joaquin River, Sacramento River, Russian River, Napa River, San Lorenzo River, Boulder Creek, Pescadero Creek, and Lagunitas Creek.

CLIMATE

The climate is mild, with long dry summers cooled near the coast by fog; warm to hot east of the north-south mountain ranges wherever the fog does not penetrate. The winters are relatively warm near the coast, but quite cool higher in the mountains and east of the

Vaca Mountains, Berkeley Hills, and Diablo Range.

For the entire area the average annual temperature is 57° F., with an average maximum of 69 and an average minimum of 46. The growing season (last killing frost to the first killing frost) varies from an average minimum of 180 days at the summit of Mount Hamilton to an average maximum of 362 days at Point Reyes.

Most of the rain falls during the winter months, with the greatest amount for a single month usually in January. Mean annual precipitation north of the bay is approximately 33 inches and south of the bay 20 inches. At Mount St. Helena mean annual precipitation reaches 59.5 inches and in the Santa Cruz Mountains 44.8 inches, but in the valleys east of the crest of Diablo Range as little as 10 to 14 inches.

Snow and hail, except on the highest peaks, are rare and unimportant in the bay region. Two important climatic factors are fog and cloud cover. Since they act as screens to reduce the amount of sunshine, they affect the temperature, rate of evaporation, and relative humidity. Fog and cloud cover seem to be necessary to some plants and of great importance to some animals, and thus these climatic factors play a part in determining the kinds and numbers of terrestrial plants and animals living in this area. The mean annual cloudiness in the bay region is between 50 and 60 per cent, with more than 70 per cent in northern Sonoma County along the coast but less than 40 percent in the inner coastal ranges.

SEASONS

Obviously the seasons of the year do not have the same meaning in the bay region that they have, for example, in New England or the Middle West. Climate alone might indicate just two seasons—wet and dry—but nature itself, through the plants and animals, gives abundant evidence of the changing seasons. However, the seasons in California can be only loosely correlated with the calendar seasons, because many of the significant seasonal events may take place from a few weeks to several months earlier or later than usual in response to climatic variations.

Spring.—The grass cover is green as spring starts, but soon turns brown (except in the foggiest areas, where it may remain green until fall) unless there are unusual spring rains. Migratory birds are enroute north, large flocks of House Finches and blackbirds break up into pairs, nesting of birds begins, and bird singing is at the peak of intensity. Mass blooming of early wild flowers is a conspicuous sign of spring. The Sara Orange-Tip and Common Checkerspot butterflies are on the wing. With warm days, lizards resume activities and insects become plentiful.

Summer.—The grass cover is now uniformly brown except near water and in areas of continuous summer fog. There is general rearing of young by resident birds. The intensity of bird songs declines as summer progresses, and migratory shore birds are on the way south by the middle or end of summer. Late-blooming wild flowers are now at their peak. The California Buckeye loses its leaves by mid-summer, and its naked, scraggly form stands out conspicuously on the hillsides until the other deciduous trees lose their leaves in the fall. Fritillaries, satyrs, and alfalfa butterflies are in flight.

Fall.—The grass cover remains brown generally and now turns brown in areas kept green by fog through the summer. Bird songs are at a minimum, with

House Finches and blackbirds again flocking. Migratory waterfowl return to the marshes and bays. Few wild flowers are blooming, but the blue blossoms of Chicory are still conspicuous along many roadsides. Coyote Brush is in full bloom along highways and on hillsides throughout much of the area. Monarch Butterflies migrate southward, and cocoons of native silk moths are formed on cherry and plum trees, wild cherry, wild lilac, and California Coffee Berry. With the first showers, two animal groups respond as if by magic. Termites invariably take off on a mating flight and start new colonies, and salamanders come out of hiding to resume activities. With heavy, soaking rains, pleocoma June beetles emerge from the ground and may be seen buzzing along in the rain less than a foot above the ground.

Winter.—In the bay region, nature's "great reawakening" usually takes place in winter rather than in spring. With the first heavy rains fresh green shoots of grass start pushing through last season's dry brown cover, and usually by mid-January central California's hills are again a lush green. Fruit orchards are soon knee-deep in grass, and many of them are carpeted a brilliant yellow with wild mustard. As the buttercups come into bloom in late winter, wild bees emerge from their cells and pollinate them. Some migratory birds reappear as early as January and February on their way north again. Some ornamental fruit trees bloom in January, "pussies" appear on willows, and the first wild flowers bloom by February. Several species of manzanita and wild currant or gooseberry blossom in January. A few warm days at any time during the winter will bring out the Mourning Cloaks, and the early "spring" butterflies emerge in February.

LIVING THINGS

Living things are usually considered to be either plants or animals. Thus every form of life is placed by most biologists in one of two major groups, the Plant Kingdom or the Animal Kingdom.

THE PLANT WORLD

We all recognize the trees, shrubs, and flowers in the garden as plants, but we might have difficulty explaining what they have in common with seaweed in the ocean, scum on a stagnant pond, or lichens on a rock. Most plants do have several characteristics in common that distinguish them from animals. These include the possession of chlorophyll that gives them their green color and makes possible the manufacture of sugar and starch, cell walls formed of a carbohydrate called cellulose, inability to move rapidly by themselves, and the inability to react quickly to stimuli. Although the more primitive plants may not have all of these characteristics, they are able to make their own food from materials obtained from the air, water, and earth.

Plants may vary from bacteria 1/250,000 of an inch across to giant redwoods 350 feet tall and 30 feet in diameter. Between these extremes are the familiar flowers and shrubs of the garden, the trees, wild flowers, ferns, and weeds of the countryside, and the less familiar algae, fungi, molds, mosses, and seaweeds.

Botanists estimate that there are between 250,000 and 350,000 different plant species known from throughout the world. These are placed in two subkingdoms—Thallophyta and Embryophyta. The Thallophyta includes bacteria, pond scums, seaweeds, molds, and mushrooms. The Embryophyta includes

[14]

The Plant Kingdom

mosses, ferns, club-mosses, conifers, and flowering plants. Representatives of some of these groups are shown on page 15.

THE ANIMAL WORLD

To many people the word "animal" is synonymous with "mammal." The term "mammal" should refer only to those warm-blooded, fur-bearing, milk-producing animals seen on the farm, in the zoo, or in the fields and forest, and including man himself (see *Mammals of the San Francisco Bay Region*). The term "animal" correctly refers to all living things that are not plants. Hence, the lion, the tiger, jelly-fish, sardine, lizard, butterfly, oyster, spider, and sparrow are all members of the Animal Kingdom and are properly called animals.

Animals vary from one-celled protozoans so small that they can be seen only with a microscope to the Blue Whale that may exceed 100 feet in length and 150 tons in weight. The squid at the bottom of the sea, the worm in the garden, and the bird in the nest are all strikingly different from each other, yet along with all other animals have certain characteristics in common. Most animals can move about rapidly at will, in contrast to plants, and are much more sensitive to external stimuli than are plants. Since animals cannot manufacture their own food, they must depend directly or indirectly on plants for their food.

Zoölogists differ in their estimates of the number of animal species in the world, with estimated totals ranging from 800,000 to 1,162,000 species. These animals are placed by most zoölogists in 22 groups, called phyla, which are divided into various subphyla, classes, and subclasses. Representatives of some of these groups are shown on page 17.

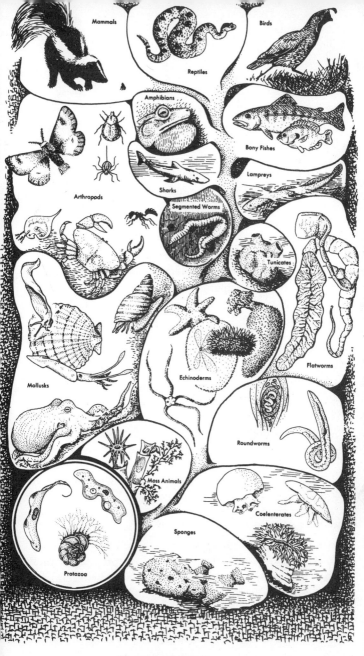

The Animal Kingdom

"What's in a name?" A very great deal, if the truth be known. If our streets were not named, we would have difficulty finding our way around in strange cities and towns. If our cities were not named and our highways numbered, we would have even more trouble finding unfamiliar cities in the first place.

Your correct name may be Robert Duncan Mac-Donald, but to your former grade school pals you may still be "Fatso" and to your old high school chums "Butch." Your mother may call you Robert Duncan, your father and close friends, Bob, but to most others you may always be just "Mac." However, only Robert Duncan MacDonald will be recognized as your full legal name.

So it is in the animal and plant world. Every different animal and plant has been given an "official" or "scientific" name. These scientific names are derived from Latin and Greek words and are recognized throughout the world. But in other countries, in various parts of this country, and even to different groups of people in the bay region, one species of animal may have any number of "common" names (just as you may be known by many nicknames). For example, you may know a certain familiar bird as the House Finch. Your friends may insist it is a Linnet, and in Mexico it may be called *Gorreón*. However, to the scientists in the United States and Mexico, and to the rest of the world, it is always *Carpodacus mexicanus*.

Some of our common ducks probably hold the record for the greatest number of popular names. The familiar Ruddy Duck is known to hunters and farmers from coast to coast by sixty-two other names.

The Mountain Lion is another well-known animal of many aliases.

In California the common names of species that occur only east of the Rocky Mountains are often mistakenly applied to some of our native plants and animals, even though they only slightly resemble the eastern species and may be but distantly related.

Sometimes the same common name may be applied to several completely different animals. In California a "gopher" is the pocket gopher—the familiar burrowing and gnawing rodent that plays havoc with our lawns and gardens. In the Great Plains, Rocky Mountains, and western Canada a "gopher" is a ground squirrel. However, in Florida a "gopher" is a land tortoise. Thus, we can readily see how great the chances for confusion are in using common names, but for each plant and animal there is only one correct scientific name.

Whether or not we learn the scientific name of a plant or animal must depend on the extent of our interest. We can certainly appreciate the beauty of a flower without learning its name, but how can we describe it properly or discuss it with someone else if we do not know the correct name?

As soon as we become sufficiently interested in some field of natural history so that we wish to continue to add to our knowledge of the subject, names become essential. For the professional worker, correct identification is the foundation on which scientific research or control programs must be based.

For some plant and animal groups (such as forest trees, birds, mammals, reptiles, and amphibians), an approved list of common names has been agreed on by specialists, so that there is no need to learn the scientific names except in the field of research.

In the California Natural History Guides, common names for species will be capitalized, but general names that refer to groups of species or one or more genera will not be capitalized. Thus, sparrow is not capitalized, but Golden-crowned Sparrow is.

Often, however, no common names exist, and the scientific names must be used. The scientific names are not really as difficult as they seem at first. They only seem difficult because they are new to us. The common names of many plants and animals are known to everyone, and yet they are actually scientific names that have become familiar through usage: Rhododendron and Eucalyptus among the plants, Rhinoceros and Hippopotamus among the animals.

The scientific name of every plant and animal is made up of two parts: the genus (plural—genera) and the species (singular and plural). The generic name is comparable to your family name and the specific name to your given name. Thus one of our familiar birds, the Western Gull, is known scientifically as *Larus occidentalis*. (In Latin *Larus* means gull and *occidentalis*, western.) In scientific writing the name, or an abbreviation of the name, of the person who first described and named the species is also included.

Since Audubon named this bird, its complete name is *Larus occidentalis* Audubon. Close relatives of the Western Gull belong to the same genus but different species. Another California representative of this genus is *Larus californicus* Lawrence, the California Gull. Note also that the genus is always capitalized, but the species is not, and that both names are italicized. In botany, specific names derived from the names of persons may sometimes be capitalized.

The complete scientific classification of the California Wild Rose is as follows:

> Kingdom: Plant
> Subkingdom: Embryophyta
> Phylum: Tracheophyta
> Subphylum: Pteropsida
> Class: Angiospermae
> Subclass: Dicotyledonae
> Order: Rosales
> Family: Rosaceae
> Genus: *Rosa*
> Species: *californica*

The scientific name of this wild rose then is *Rosa californica* C. & S.

The complete classification for the Norway Rat is as shown:

> Kingdom: Animal
> Subkingdom: Metazoa
> Phylum: Chordata
> Subphylum: Gnathostomata
> Class: Mammalia
> Order: Rodentia
> Family: Muridae
> Genus: *Rattus*
> Species: *norvegicus*

The scientific name of this rat is *Rattus norvegicus* (Erxleben).

BIOTIC COMMUNITIES
OF THE BAY REGION

In driving about the bay region you will notice that certain birds are usually found in the same kind of place. For instance, the Western Winter Wren nearly always gives its tinkling song from the deep woods, the Western Meadowlark proclaims the glory of the day from a fence post at the edge of a meadow, and the American Egret is seen stalking in the marshes. Observation will show that butterflies also restrict themselves to certain areas: the Woodland Satyr may be found in oak woodlands, the Editha Checkerspot flying over barren hills, and the Satyr Anglewing darting from tree to tree along a wooded stream. Further observation will also show that certain trees, shrubs, flowers, and other plants usually occur together.

Biologists noticed these associations of plants and animals many years ago and developed the "life zone" concept to account for the distribution of plant and animal species in association with each other. However, life zones are based primarily on temperature

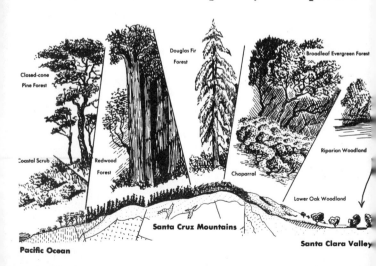

differences, and it is now known that plant and animal distribution is far too complex to be determined fully by any single environmental factor. Animal distribution may be affected by many factors, including available breeding habitats, available shelter, competition, soil moisture and acidity, light, cloudiness, rain, atmospheric density, humidity, altitude, food, and vegetation as well as temperature.

In order to account more adequately for the occurrence of certain plant and animal species in natural communities, many biologists in recent years have classified areas of plant and animal distribution in other ways. The most useful classification for the naturalist in California is one based on vegetation zones or plant communities. A classification of the biotic communities of the bay region is presented on the following pages. It should be emphasized that these communities are not always distinct since they frequently merge into each other, but the elements are usually recognizable. (For illustrations typical of the biotic communities described in the following table, see pages 33–40.)

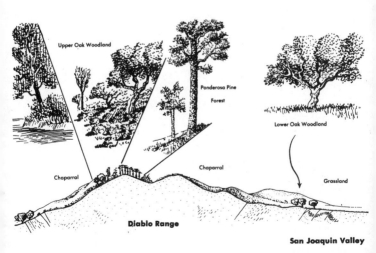

COMMUNITY	LOCATIONS AND EXAMPLES
1. Rocky Shore	Rocky beaches, mostly subject to wave and tide action, along coast in Sonoma, Marin, San Francisco, San Mateo, Santa Cruz counties. Examples—north end of Moss Beach, San Mateo County.
2. Coastal Strand	Sandy beaches, dunes along coast in Sonoma, Marin, San Francisco, San Mateo, Santa Cruz counties. Examples—Stinson Beach; Rockaway Beach.
3. Coastal Salt Marsh	Salt marshes along coast in Sonoma, Marin, San Mateo, Santa Cruz counties; along bay shore in San Mateo, Santa Clara, Alameda, Marin, Napa, Contra Costa, Solano counties. Examples—Alviso marshes; Audubon sanctuary along south bay shores.
4. Freshwater Marsh	Scattered areas along coast, in back of salty areas. Around springs, ponds, along sluggish streams in Santa Clara, Contra Costa, Napa, Solano counties. Examples—Searsville Lake; Bear Creek near Point Reyes Station.

CHARACTERISTIC PLANTS	CHARACTERISTIC ANIMALS
Surf grasses (*Phyllospadix Torreyi* and *P. Scouleri*), numerous marine plants.	Black Turnstone (*Arenaria melanocephala*), Surfbird (*Aphriza virgata*), Wandering Tattler (*Heteroscelus incanum*), great variety of invertebrates.
Tree Lupine (*Lupinus arboreus*), Sea Rocket (*Cakile edentula*), a blue grass (*Poa douglasi*), sand verbena (*Abronia* spp.), Beach Grass (*Ammophila arenaria*).	Sanderling (*Crocethia alba*), Snowy Plover (*Charadrius alexandrinus*), a sand crab (*Emerita analoga*), a rove beetle (*Thinopinus pictus*), beach amphipods or "fleas" (*Orchestia traskiana, Orchestoidea* spp.).
Pickle-weed (*Salicornia ambigua*), Sea Blite (*Suaeda californica*), Marsh Rosemary (*Limonium commune*), Marsh Grindelia (*Grindelia cuneifolia*), Calif. Cord Grass (*Spartina foliosa*).	Clapper Rail (*Rallus longirostris*), Marsh Hawk (*Circus cyaneus*), Short-eared Owl (*Asio flammeus*), Salt-marsh Harvest Mouse (*Reithrodontomys raviventris*), Vagrant Shrew (*Sorex vagrans*), a salt marsh fly (*Ephydra riparia*), salt marsh mosquitoes (*Aedes squamiger, A. dorsalis*).
Common Tule (*Scirpus acutus*), Calif. Bulrush (*Scirpus californicus*), Common Cat-tail (*Typha latifolia*), sedge (*Carex senta* and other spp.).	Long-billed Marsh Wren (*Telmatodytes palustris*), Redwinged Blackbird (*Agelaius phoeniceus*), Yellowthroat (*Geothlypis trichas*), garter snakes (*Thamnophis* spp.), Pacific Tree Frog (*Hyla regilla*), predaceous diving beetles (*Dytiscus* spp.), a water scavenger beetle (*Hydrophilus triangularis*), a giant water bug (*Lethocerus americanus*).

COMMUNITY	LOCATIONS AND EXAMPLES
5. Coastal Scrub	Dry rocky or gravelly slopes from Napa to Santa Clara County mostly below 3,000 ft. and below chaparral; also from Sonoma to Santa Cruz County on slopes or in canyons facing the coast. Examples—steep slopes along Hwy. 1 in Marin County.
6. Closed-cone Pine Forest	Interrupted forest on seaward side of the redwoods, from near sea level to 1,200 ft. Sonoma, Marin, San Mateo, Santa Cruz counties. Examples—Tomales Bay State Park and hills near Año Nuevo Point.
7. Redwood Forest	Slopes from 10 to 2,000 ft. in Sonoma, Marin, Alameda, San Mateo, Santa Clara, Santa Cruz counties. Examples—Muir Woods; Big Basin; San Mateo County Memorial Park; Samuel P. Taylor State Park.
8. Douglas Fir Forest	Scattered patches in Sonoma, Marin, San Mateo, Santa Cruz counties both east and west of the redwoods. Examples—Inverness Ridge.
9. Ponderosa Pine Forest	Small area on Howell Mountain in Napa County and scattered patches elsewhere in Sonoma, Santa Cruz, Santa Clara counties. Examples—Howell Mountain.

CHARACTERISTIC PLANTS	CHARACTERISTIC ANIMALS
California Sage Brush (*Artemisia californica*), Black Sage (*Salvia mellifera*), Coyote Brush (*Baccharis pilularis*), Bush Monkeyflower (*Diplacus aurantiacus*).	Rufous-crowned Sparrow (*Aimophila ruficeps*), Rock Wren (*Salpinctes obsoletus*), Wrentit (*Chamaea fasciata*), Brush Rabbit (*Sylvilagus bachmani*), Western Fence Lizard (*Sceloporus occidentalis*).
Bishop Pine (*Pinus muricata*), Monterey Pine (*P. radiata*).	Pygmy Nuthatch (*Sitta pygmaea*), Western Pine Engraver (*Ips plastographus*), Monterey Pine Aphis (*Essigella californica*), Monterey Pine Midge (*Thecodiplosis piniradiatae*).
Coast Redwood (*Sequoia sempervirens*), Douglas Fir (*Pseudotsuga taxifolia*), Wax Myrtle (*Myrica californica*), Redwood Sorrel (*Oxalis oregona*), Thimble Berry (*Rubus parviflora*), Calif. Sword Fern (*Polystichum munitum*).	Winter Wren (*Troglodytes troglodytes*), Mountain Beaver (*Aplodontia rufa*) (north of bay), Trowbridge Shrew (*Sorex trowbridgei*), Pacific Giant Salamander (*Dicamptodon ensatus*), Ensatina (*Ensatina eschscholtzi*).
Douglas Fir (*P. taxifolia*), Tanoak (*Lithocarpus densiflora*), Madrone (*Arbutus menziesi*), Calif. Laurel (*Umbellularia californica*).	Brown Creeper (*Certhia familiaris*), Golden-crowned Kinglet (*Regulus satrapa*), Western Gray Squirrel (*Sciurus griseus*), Dusky-footed Wood Rat (*Neotoma fuscipes*), Douglas Fir Bark Beetle (*Dendroctonus pseudotsugae*).
Ponderosa Pine (*Pinus ponderosa*), Calif. Black Oak (*Quercus kelloggi*).	Pileated Woodpecker (*Dryocopus pileatus*), Pine Sawyer (*Ergates spiculatus*).

COMMUNITY	LOCATIONS AND EXAMPLES
10. Broadleaf Evergreen Forest	On higher hills within the redwood forest and along its inner edge at elevations from 200 to 2,500 ft.; in Sonoma, Marin, Santa Cruz counties; in Diablo Range in Contra Costa, Alameda, Santa Clara counties. Examples—Jasper Ridge near Palo Alto.
11. Oak Woodland	Inner coastal ranges from 400 to 3,000 ft.; Napa, Solano, Contra Costa, Alameda, Santa Clara counties. Examples—rolling hills along both edges of Santa Clara Valley and along Hwy. 101 in Marin County.
12. Chaparral	Higher dry slopes and ridges generally throughout the area. Examples—large areas found on Mount Diablo, Mount Tamalpais, and in the Santa Cruz Mountains.

CHARACTERISTIC PLANTS	CHARACTERISTIC ANIMALS
Tanoak (*Lithocarpus densiflora*), Calif. Laurel (*Umbellularia californica*), Madrone (*Arbutus menziesi*), Calif. Buckeye (*Aesculus californica*), Golden Chinquapin (*Castanopsis chrysophylla minor*), Coast Live Oak (*Quercus agrifolia*), Douglas Fir (*Pseudotsuga taxifolia*).	Black-headed Grosbeak (*Pheucticus melanocephalus*), Hutton's Vireo (*Vireo huttoni*), Western Gray Squirrel (*Sciurus griseus*), Dusky-footed Wood Rat (*Neotoma fuscipes*), Calif. Slender Salamander (*Batrachoseps attenuatus*), Arboreal Salamander (*Aneides lugubris*), Calif. Laurel Borer (*Rosalia funebris*).
At lower elevations: Valley Oak (*Quercus lobata*), Coast Live Oak (*Q. agrifolia*). At higher elevations: Blue Oak (*Q. douglasi*), Digger Pine (*Pinus sabiniana*). Throughout: Holly-leaf Cherry (*Prunus ilicifolia*), Calif. Coffee Berry (*Rhamnus californica*), Calif. Buckeye (*A. californica*), Poison Oak (*Rhus diversiloba*).	Acorn woodpecker (*Melanerpes formicivorus*), White-breasted Nuthatch (*Sitta carolinensis*), Brush Mouse (*Peromyscus boylei*), Calif. Ground Squirrel (*Citellus beecheyi*), Calif. Sister (*Heterochroa californica*), Calif. Oak Moth (*Phryganidea californica*), Calif. Prionus (*Prionus californicus*).
Chamise (*Adenostoma fasciculatum*), Scrub Oak (*Q. dumosa*), Holly-leaf Cherry (*P. ilicifolia*), Buckbrush (*Ceanothus cuneatus*), Calif. Coffee Berry (*R. californica*), manzanita (*Arctostaphylos* spp.), wild lilac (*Ceonothus* spp.).	Bewick's Wren (*Thryomanes bewicki*), Wrentit (*Chamaea fasciata*), Calif. Thrasher (*Toxostoma redivivum*), **North of Bay**—Sonoma Chipmunk (*Eutamias sonomae*), **South of Bay**—Merriam Chipmunk (*E. merriami*), Striped Racer (*Masticophis lateralis*), Gray Hairstreak (*Strymon adenostomatis*).

COMMUNITY	LOCATIONS AND EXAMPLES
13. Grassland	Scattered bits of coastal prairie on hills or in glades along the coast; scattered remnants of valley grassland in coastal valleys of Napa, Alameda, and Santa Clara counties and in the Great Central Valley which enters our area in Solano County and the northeastern tip of Contra Costa County. Examples—Point Reyes and noncultivated areas in Livermore Valley and adjacent hills.
14. Riparian Woodland	Throughout the area in wooded canyons and along valley watercourses where not destroyed by man. [A] In drier interior ranges of Santa Clara, Alameda, Contra Costa, and Napa counties. Examples—Pacheco Creek Canyon and Alum Rock Canyon. [B] In ranges west of Santa Clara Valley, north of San Francisco Bay, and in moister canyons of the northern Diablo Range. Examples— Pescadero Creek Canyon.
15. Rural	Cultivated crop lands and pasture lands; mostly in Santa Clara, Santa Cruz, Solano, Napa, Sonoma, eastern Contra Costa, and eastern Alameda counties.
16. Urban	Cities, towns, and subdivisions enclosing parks, cemeteries, vacant lots, and some extensive eucalyptus forests.

CHARACTERISTIC PLANTS	CHARACTERISTIC ANIMALS
Blue Bunch Grass (*Festuca idahoensis*), Calif. Oat Grass (*Danthonia californica*), Foothill Sedge (*Carex tumulicola*), brome grass (*Bromus* spp.), wild oats (*Avena* spp.).	Western Meadowlark (*Sturnella neglecta*), Horned Lark (*Eremophila alpestris*), Calif. Ground Squirrel (*Citellus beecheyi*), Black-tailed Jack Rabbit (*Lepus californicus*), Calif. Vole (*Microtus californicus*), Gopher Snake (*Pituophis catenifer*), Field Cricket (*Acheta assimilis*).
[A] Western Sycamore (*Platanus racemosa*), Fremont Cottonwood (*Populus fremonti*), Red Willow (*Salix laevigata*), Arroyo Willow (*S. lasiolepis*). [B] Boxelder (*Acer negundo*), Big Leaf Maple (*A. macrophyllum*), White Alder (*Alnus rhombifolia*), Red Alder (*A. rubra*) (restricted to within 30 miles of the coast).	Downy Woodpecker (*Dendrocopos pubescens*), Yellow Warbler (*Dendroica petechia*), Yellow-breasted Chat (*Icteria virens*), Raccoon (*Procyon lotor*), Western Pond Turtle (*Clemmys marmorata*), Calif. Newt (*Taricha torosa*), Lorquin's Admiral (*Basilarchia lorquini*), Mourning Cloak (*Nymphalis antiopa*), Box Elder Bug (*Leptocoris trivitattus*), Spotted Tree Borer (*Synaphaeta guexi*).
Alfalfa, truck crops, prune, apricot, pear, grape vines, eucalyptus, willows, and poplars.	Barn Owl (*Tyto alba*), Sparrow Hawk (*Falco sparverius*), Brewer's Blackbird (*Euphagus cyanocephalus*), Botta Pocket Gopher (*Thomomys bottae*), Calif. Vole (*M. californicus*), Gopher Snake (*P. catenifer*), Alfalfa Butterfly (*Colias eurytheme*), Cabbage Butterfly (*Pieris rapae*).
Great variety of introduced trees, shrubs, and garden flowers.	House Finch (*Carpodacus mexicanus*), English Sparrow (*Passer domesticus*), Norway Rat (*Rattus norvegicus*), House Mouse (*Mus musculus*), American Cockroach (*Periplanata americana*).

THE COMMUNITY OF NATURE

Our human communities, whether urban or rural, are very highly organized. Lumbermen, carpenters, masons, plumbers, and others work to provide shelter. Farmers raise crops for bakers, butchers, canners, and frozen-food plants to process as food for our table. Still others provide the materials that go to make up our clothing. In addition, there are numerous trades and professions to satisfy the many needs and desires of the human community. In this human society a state of interdependence and delicate equilibrium has been reached. The balance is not stable, however, but shifts constantly with changes in the community. Thus a strike in a major industry, a devastating flood or earthquake, or prolonged drought can have a profound effect on the lives of farmers, bakers, carpenters, and office workers.

It is the same, though more direct, in the world of nature. In nature, plants serve as food for animals, animals serve as a food supply for other animals, insects and rodents till the soil, vultures, scavenger beetles, and blow flies provide community sanitation, predators and disease agents prevent overpopulation, and every other plant and animal fills a niche of its own. This community organization in nature has variously been called the chain or web of life, the balance of nature, or a biological complex.

For instance, we might speak of the biological complex dependent on a single plant species. On page 42 we see a complex showing some of the different plants and animals that depend directly or indirectly on the oak tree for their existence. A single "chain" from an animal at the end of the line (see p. 42) back to its beginning, in this case some part

Rocky Shore

Coastal Strand

Coastal Salt Marsh

Freshwater Marsh
(Broadleaf Evergreen Forest in background)

Coastal Scrub
(Closed-cone Pine Forest in background)

Closed-cone Pine Forest

Redwood Forest

Ponderosa Pine Forest

*Douglas Fir
Forest*

*Broadleaf
Evergreen
Forest*

*Oak
Woodland*

Chaparral

Grassland

*Riparian Woodland (Oak Woodland on hill at left;
Coastal Scrub in distance)*

Rural

Urban

of the oak tree, is called a *food chain*.

When man fails to understand this interdependence of living things he frequently upsets the equilibrium in his attempts to rearrange nature to suit himself. In the oak complex, for example, man may be annoyed by the excessive number of California Oak Moth caterpillars that destroy the foliage and then crawl into his house. He may decide to spray his oak trees and thus destroy this insect pest. However, if he chooses one of the new deadly contact sprays that kills everything that crawls across the leaves, instead of a stomach poison to kill only what eats the leaves, he will also destroy the many parasites and predators which normally keep this moth in check. The chemical chosen may be more efficient in killing the predators and parasites than in destroying the moth itself. Then, when the moth population builds back up, there are fewer natural enemies to control it, and the man and his oak trees are worse off than ever.

If man does not take into account the laws of nature, he can do irreparable damage to the natural community. The farmer who kills off the hawks and owls may find that he has shifted the natural balance so that his fields are overrun with ground squirrels and mice. Wildlife workers have found that if the natural enemies of deer are exterminated, deer populations will increase greatly, eat up all available food, and then die of starvation or destroy man's crops or garden plants.

An extreme example of this is seen in the introduction of nonnative species to a new habitat without competent scientific supervision. Rabbits, after introduction into Australia, went on a population "explosion." They were no longer controlled by natural checks (predators), and soon became a major pest

Biological interrelationships in an Oak Complex

1
Golden
Eagle

72 Foxes

Approximately 100,000 White-footed Mice

Millions of seeds, berries, and insects

Pyramid of Numbers, showing the numbers of animals supported on eighteen square miles of land.

over thousands of miles. Many major insect pests are "escapees" that have been introduced accidentally from other countries. Among these "undesirable aliens" are the Cotton Boll Weevil from Mexico, Cabbage Butterfly from Europe, and the Khapra Beetle from Asia.

The numbers of animals of various kinds that can be supported under natural circumstances in a given area are determined by all of the interrelationships within the biological complex (see p. 42). Biologists call this the *pyramid of numbers*. Stated simply, this means that it may take tremendous numbers of plant-eating insects to feed a shrew, large numbers of shrews to support a small carnivore such as a weasel, but fewer weasels to support a Great Horned Owl at the top of this food chain. For an example of another pyramid of numbers, see page 43. Nature supports this arrangement by supplying a high *biotic potential,* or capacity to reproduce, to the animals or plants at the bottom of the pyramid and a low biotic potential to those at the top.

NATURE ACTIVITIES

There are many ways to enjoy the out-of-doors. For some it is sufficient merely to appreciate the fresh spring beauty of a mariposa lily, to admire a newly emerged swallowtail butterfly, or to marvel at the kaleidoscopic color reflected from the throat of a hummingbird. For others it will be enough to learn to recognize (by sight or, sometimes, sound) the bay region plants and animals of interest.

Still others may wish to devote more time and effort to nature study, and for them there is a wealth of varied activities from which to choose. Some of these activities are described below. Further information can be obtained from William Hillcourt's *Field Book of Nature Activities* (New York: Putnam, 1961) and Elizabeth K. Cooper's *Science in Your Own Backyard* (New York: Harcourt, Brace and World, 1958).

LOOKING AT NATURE

This method of enjoying nature can be just as strenuous or sedentary, expensive or economical, or complex or simple as desired. Essentially, looking at nature is what Thoreau did at Walden, Burroughs did in New York, and Muir did in the High Sierra.

The only equipment necessary for this activity, in its simplest form, is an inquiring mind and a sharp pair of eyes. Soon, however, you will want to know the names of the things you see, and for that you will need guide books on specific subjects. As you gain experience and perhaps become specialized in your interest, you will want to add special equipment—binoculars for bird watching, a hand lens for insect or plant study, a geologist's hammer, and so on.

One of the advantages of looking at nature is that

you need not go far afield to enjoy this activity. There is much to be seen right in your own backyard or in the vacant lot down the street. (See Audubon Training, "How To Explore Nature in the City," address on p. 66.)

Writing about Nature

Your written observations on nature can be as brief or as complete as you wish, depending on your purpose. Your writing can be as simple as keeping a "life list" or indicating on a check list the species seen on each field trip. The bird watchers' life list has been very popular, and is merely a list of the birds personally seen (preferably with uncertain identifications verified by an expert), with a record of the date and place first seen. The life list is also used now by enthusiasts in other fields of natural history.

Some bird clubs have printed check lists of local birds for field trip use. Information on the availability of these lists can be obtained from the National Audubon Society, Western Representative (address on p. 66). Detailed check lists of plants, reptiles, amphibians, and mammals for certain localities are found in many of the scientific and popular books on the flora and fauna of California.

Thoreau, Burroughs, and Muir did not rely on their memories to recall what they saw, but kept detailed records of their nature observations. To see how major literary contributions in natural history can be based on daily journals of nature observations, see Aldo Leopold's *Sand County Almanac* (New York: Oxford, 1966.)

For more extensive note taking, index cards, looseleaf or bound notebooks, or diaries can be used. Choice will depend on your note-taking habits and the use you wish to make of your notes. Many naturalists and professional biologists who observe nature do so according to a prearranged plan and with a definite scientific purpose in mind. They keep careful records of everything they see in nature, writing their notes as they observe or each night.

The important thing is to write down exactly what you see as objectively as possible. If you want others to respect your records, you must make accurate observations. Then, if you discover something new to science, your observations will be accepted as a scientific contribution rather than rejected as unreliable. In this age of advanced science, many people seem to think that all the basic facts about the birds, the flowers, and other plants and animals are known, but this' is far from true. The unknown about nature is much greater than the known.

Only in recent years have we solved, through careful observations, the mysteries of how bees communicate with each other, how bats in flight avoid hitting objects in the dark, and how far a fly can fly. But we still do not know the basic life histories of many of the insects, birds, mammals, reptiles, amphibians, and other animals right here in the bay region. In the field of natural history there are indeed exceptional opportunities for worthwhile contributions from the amateur.

READING ABOUT NATURE

Your appreciation of and interest in nature can be greatly increased through reading. Excellent introductions to the pleasure of reading about nature are John Kieran's *Treasury of Great Nature Writing* (Garden City: Hanover House, 1957), Roger T. Peterson's *The Bird Watcher's Anthology* (New York:

Harcourt, Brace, 1957), and Charles Neider's *The Fabulous Insects* (New York: Harper, 1954).

Printed lists of natural history books can be obtained by writing to Eric Lundberg (Ashton, Md. 20702), Pierce Book Company (Winthrop, Iowa 50682), or to Julian J. Nadolny (35 Varmor Drive, New Britain, Conn. 06053). New nature books are reviewed regularly in San Francisco's *Chronicle* and *Examiner*. For out-of-print and new nature books, consult advertisements in *Audubon* magazine, *National Wildlife* magazine, and *Natural History* magazine.

Besides the special works on nature mentioned throughout this book, there is a selected list of suggested reading references on pages 71-72. For additional suggestions, consult your local bookstore or library.

PHOTOGRAPHING NATURE

If you wish to relive memorable experiences afield but do not care for acquiring a specimen collection, photography can form an ideal adjunct to your nature hobby or supply a hobby interest all its own.

With an inexpensive box camera, you can make satisfactory pictures of physiographic land forms (such as mountains, valleys, streams, and volcanic cones), clouds (with a filter), typical habitats for various animals, and types of vegetation.

For sharp photographs of birds, mammals, reptiles, insects, or wild flowers, you will need at least a moderately expensive camera with a good lens and shutter, bellows extension or focusing lens mount, and preferably ground-glass focusing. For photographic specialties, such as photomicrography, high-speed photography, color photography, or cinematography, additional equipment will be required.

Helpful and interesting references are Russ Kinne's *Complete Book of Nature Photography* (New York: A. S. Barnes, 1965), Sam Dunton's *Guide to Photographing Animals* (New York: Greenberg, 1956), and Edward S. Ross' *Insects Close Up* (Berkeley: University of California Press, 1953). For the latest information on nature photography, see frequent articles in photography and nature magazines and various booklets by the Eastman Kodak Company.

SKETCHING NATURE

As you sit by the trail and observe chipmunks at work and play, you may wish to capture their characteristic appearance with a pencil. A small sketching pad will fit in your field kit or pocket. Although your sketches may never have the professional look of a drawing by William D. Berry (see *Mammals of the San Francisco Bay Region*), they will improve with practice and will greatly enhance the value of your nature notes. Birds, mammals, insects, flowers, and trees are all likely subjects for your sketches. You may also want to prepare a vegetation map of a habitat you are studying or sketch in the habitual routes taken by various birds, bees, or butterflies as they go about their daily activities.

To help you get started with your sketching, you can take one of the drawing courses offered by your local adult evening school, YWCA, or YMCA, or you can consult a book on sketching. Good books on nature drawing include Papp: *Scientific Illustration* (Dubuque: Wm. C. Brown, 1968); Zweifel: *Handbook of Biological Illustration* (Chicago: University of Chicago Press, 1965); and Knudsen: *Biological Techniques* (New York: Harper & Row, 1966).

The "pack rat" instinct is strong in most of us, and many people first become interested in nature through carrying an interesting-looking sea shell, rock, or pine cone home from a Sunday outing. There is no better way to study certain fields of natural history than by making a nature collection. If the "rules and regulations" of science are followed, your collection can be not only a source of much pleasure to you, but also a "storehouse" of valuable scientific information of interest to others as well.

There is no limit to the variety of nature objects that can be collected and studied. Some of the specimens commonly collected are:

Butterflies, beetles, and other insects
Wild flowers, leaves, pine cones, and wood samples
Sea shells and other specimens from beach and tide pool
Animal tracks in plaster casts
Rocks, minerals, soil samples, and fossils
Indian relics such as arrowheads, stone mortars and pestles.

Experienced collectors frequently exchange their duplicate specimens with others. *The Naturalists' Directory* (International) (PCL Publications, Box 282, Phillipsburg, N.J.) lists natural history collectors from all over the world, their subjects of interest, and what they have to exchange.

Bring Them Back Alive

Many of the animals you find in the field are best left right there. In fact, it may be a violation of state game or health laws to capture certain mammals and birds, and it does not make much sense to collect living rattlesnakes unless you are an experienced herpetologist and have a good reason for doing so.

However, if you are seriously interested in establishing a home zoo, there are many mammals, reptiles, amphibians, and fishes, as well as a multitude of insects and related creatures, that can supply you with many hours of pleasure both as "zoo keeper" and naturalist-observer. A word of caution: never bring home a living animal of any kind unless you intend to care for it properly or to prepare it immediately as a

specimen for your collection. Never bring home plant or animal species that are rare in your area or that are protected by law. A few suggestions for home zoo projects are:

1. Aquarium—may include tropical or native fishes or tide-pool animals.

2. Terrarium—may contain sand for lizards and snakes or moss for salamanders. Many insects also do well in the terrarium. Doodle bugs (ant lion larvae) are especially interesting to observe in captivity.

3. Ant or termite colonies and bee hives do very well in observation nests or hives, and a well-cared-for colony may last for years.

4. A collection of butterfly chrysalids and moth pupae provides a great deal of excitement when the colorful adults emerge in the spring.

For additional information, see Clifford B. Moore's *The Book of Wild Pets* (Boston: Branford, 1954), and Esther L. Guthrie's *Home Book of Animal Care* (New York: Harper and Row, 1966).

FINDING THE NAME

Perhaps the simplest way to identify plants and animals is to go into the field with an expert, have him point them out in their natural habitats, and tell you their names and characteristics. Much help can be obtained on field trips of your local nature groups. Colleges and universities offer extension courses that consist of bay area natural history field trips. Also, some state, regional, and city parks offer nature talks and walks along special trails with signs to identify the nature features.

Some plants and animals can be collected and compared with identified museum specimens or with specimens illustrated in guide books. The museum specimen or illustration most closely resembling the collected specimen is found by careful search. After arriving at this tentative identification, a comparison of the size, form, color, anatomy, and range of the museum specimen or book entry with the specimen in hand may be sufficient to give it a name. This method can be used successfully for distinctive species and for those with but few close relatives in the bay region.

To identify some specimens, however, we must make use of artificial devices called identification keys. These keys use characteristics (usually anatomical) arranged in lettered or numbered couplets. By progressively choosing the characteristic that correctly applies to the specimen in hand (or perched in the bush), you arrive at your destination—the correct

name of the specimen. A *numbered* key for certain familiar objects is given below.

1. Objects made of wood; w/wo metal parts 2
– Objects made of glass 5
2. Possessing legs 3
– Without legs 4
3. With four legs and a large, rectangular,
   flat top; without metal parts . . . . *table*
– With three legs and a small, circular,
   flat top; with metal parts . . . . . *camera tripod*
4. Large, with a series of parallel,
   horizontal boards . . . . *bookshelf*
– Small, enclosed on all six sides; with
   one side capable of being opened . . . . *cigar box*
5. Transparent . . . . *window*
– Opaque, silvered on one side . . . . *mirror*

To use the above key for identifying one of the pictured objects, choose one of the descriptions in the first couplet. Depending on your choice, you will then proceed to couplet 2 or 5 and repeat the process. When you reach a description with a name opposite it, you have "keyed" or identified your object.

A simple *lettered* key for identifying major insect groups might read, in part, as follows:

A   With two wings (one pair) . . . . *Flies*
AA With four wings (two pairs) . . . . . . B or BB
   B   Fore wings hard and leathery; without
       veins . . . . *Beetles*
   BB All four wings of equal consistency and
       veined . . . . C or CC
      C   Wings covered with tiny scales;
         mouthparts modified into a long
         tube for sucking that is coiled
         beneath the head . . *butterflies* & *moths*
      CC Wings without scales; clear and
         membranous . . . . *ants, bees,* or *wasps*

Many natural history books contain identification keys of this kind. Some keys also include drawings of the key characters. An extensive series of popular identification manuals using keys with drawings (though some emphasize primarily eastern forms) is the *Pictured Key Nature Series,* edited by H. E. Jacques (Wm. C. Brown Company, Dubuque, Iowa).

NATURE AT NIGHT

The study of nature might seem to be a daytime activity (except for stargazing), but the plants and animals are also present at night, and many animals are much more active after dark. Some college courses include a twenty-four-hour field trip so that the activities of nature can be seen in one place throughout a full day and night.

Many mammals, amphibians, and insects, as well as some reptiles and birds, can best be observed during darkness. Thus the call notes of owls, nighthawks, and frogs may make the evening interesting, and the predawn chorus of song birds in the spring offers a concert that, once experienced, is never forgotten.

Many animals can be identified at night by their "eye shine." If you attach a miner's lantern to your head or hold a flashlight near your eyes but pointed ahead along the trail, you will be surprised at the number of animals encountered on a nocturnal hike through the woods and across the fields.

For more information on nature at night, see Lorus J. and Margery J. Milne's *The World of Night* (New York: Viking, 1956).

NATURE CLUBS

If there are several people in your neighborhood who are interested in natural history, you may wish to bring them together to form a club. Club members can get together to exchange information and specimens, listen to guest speakers, show nature movies or slides, or take group field trips.

A natural history club may be made up of those interested in a single phase of nature, such as rock and mineral hunting, cactus growing, or butterfly collecting. Or it may include members interested in any and all nature activities. Any nature organization, however, should investigate the benefits offered to clubs becoming chapters or affiliates of the National Audubon Society (address on p. 66).

NATURE CRAFTS

For the do-it-yourself fan there are many worthwhile nature projects. These might include making such articles as trays or lampshades using butterflies or wild flowers; butterfly mobiles; table decorations from driftwood, cactus skeleton, or other odd-shaped woods; centerpieces from autumn weeds and leaves; leaf prints with ink, smoke, blueprint, or photo paper; plaster casts of animal tracks; bird houses and feeding stations; a miniature planetarium; or a home weather station. Many of these projects have been described in *Sunset* magazine and in various publications of the Boy Scouts and Girl Scouts as well as in general books on nature.

NATURE'S SOUNDS AND MUSIC

Just as the bird watcher soon learns to identify each bird by its song or call note, the herpetologist learns the spring serenade of each frog and the entomologist the sounds of crickets, grasshoppers, and cicadas.

If you are musically inclined, you may wish to set these sounds of nature to music or make up rhymes in imitation of the songs to help you remember them.

A growing hobby is recording nature's music. Many records are now available (some from the Houghton Mifflin Co., Boston) of the bird, frog, and insect songs recorded by Arthur A. Allen and Paul Kellogg of Cornell University and their colleagues who have pioneered this fascinating phase of natural history.

NATURE GAMES AND PLAYS

A very popular nature activity, particularly with young children, is the playing of games based on the common plants, animals, and rocks. These can be as simple as a modification of the old favorite, "I Spy," or as elaborate as a one-act play. Nature games can be played by any number in almost any situation, indoors or outdoors. Games using nature materials and plays with nature or conservation themes can provide added interest for school or camp programs.

INTERPRETING THE FACE OF THE EARTH

Scientists call this "physiography." With a knowledge of this subject, a ride through, or flight over, the bay region can be much more meaningful and enjoyable. By learning the proper "signs," you can locate earthquake fault lines, long-extinct volcanic cones, or determine that certain mountain peaks were once at the bottom of the sea.

ROCK COLLECTING

One of the most popular nature hobbies is that of collecting rocks and minerals. In the bay region there are many good collecting localities. Advanced collectors cut and polish their own stones and make them into various articles of jewelry. A helpful source of information on this hobby is Vinson Brown and David Allan's *Rocks and Minerals of California and Their Stories* (Healdsburg: Naturegraph Co., 1955).

EXPLORING CAVES

"Spelunking," as cave exploring is commonly known, has gained increased popularity in recent years. Speleologists (or spelunkers) study the geology and biology of caves as well as explore them. Cave exploring, however, should not be undertaken by the novice except in the company of an experienced spelunker who will take all necessary safety precautions.

Speleological publications list approximately a dozen caves for the bay region. Information on cave exploring can be obtained from the National Speleological Society, 1407 Hickory Court, Broyhill Park, Falls Church, Virginia. Two books for those interested in this nature hobby are Franklin Folsom's *Exploring American Caves* (New York: Collier, 1956) and Charles E. Mohr and Howard N. Sloane's *Celebrated American Caves* (New Brunswick: Rutgers University Press, 1955).

DIGGING INTO THE PAST

If you are curious about what it was like in the bay region before modern civilization, you may enjoy delving into archaeology (the study of early civilizations through relics) or paleontology (the study of fossils). The principal study tools for these activities are a pick and shovel. There are good fossil collecting sites in the bay area, and archaeological artifacts turn up occasionally. Information on paleontology is available in Simpson's *Life of the Past: An Introduction to Paleontology* (New Haven: Yale University Press, 1953), Casanova's *An Illustrated Guide to Fossil Collecting* (Healdsburg: Naturegraph Co., 1957), and Mathews' *Fossils* (New York: Golden Press, 1962).

THROUGH THE MICROSCOPE

Most of us are vaguely aware that tiny organisms, too small to be seen by the naked eye, exist all around us and indeed within our own bodies. This does not really mean very much to us though, until we actually see some of these simple plants and animals greatly enlarged by a microscope. A single drop of water from a murky pond can provide a fascinating botanical and zoölogical garden in miniature. If you have a microscope or are able to borrow one, you can explore this microscopic world. For additional information, see Julian D. Corrington's *Exploring with Your Microscope* (New York: McGraw-Hill, 1957), and Johnson and Bleifeld's *Hunting With the Microscope* (New York: Sentinel Books, 1963).

PREDICTING THE WEATHER

If you ever got soaked in a downpour after the weatherman predicted sunshine, or felt foolish with umbrella and overshoes on a beautiful day when the forecast called for rain, you might be interested in learning just what is involved in preparing a weather forecast. You can learn to read weather maps, take barometer readings, and measure precipitation and wind velocity. You may wish to set up your own weather station and then see how your forecasts compare with those in the newspaper. Valuable sources of information on weather include Irving P. Krick and Roscoe Fleming's *Sun, Sea and Sky* (Philadelphia: Lippincott, 1954), Frank Forrester's *1001 Questions Answered About the Weather* (New York: Grosset, 1957,) and Charles and Ruth Laird's *Weathercasting* (New York: Prentice-Hall, 1955).

BEACHCOMBING

For a hobby that combines exercise and fun, beachcombing is hard to beat. It is especially rewarding just after a storm. Many interesting nature treasures, such as sea shells and driftwood, can then be found washed ashore on the ocean beach. References include Sunset's *Beachcombers' Guide to the Pacific Coast* (Menlo Park: Lane Books, 1966) and Joel W. Hedgpeth's *Introduction to the Seashore Life of the San Francisco Bay Region and the Coast of Northern California* (Berkeley: University of California Press, 1962).

SKIN AND SCUBA DIVING

Probably the fastest-growing nature hobby is skin and scuba diving. Many divers are interested only in the sport, but when diving one can also learn much about underwater plant and animal life. See North: *The Golden Guide to Scuba Diving* (New York: Golden Press, 1968).

It would probably take years to exhaust the possibilities for enjoyable nature study right in your own neighborhood, but if you are like most of us you will soon want to do some nature exploring farther afield. You may wish to join with others of similar interests on regularly scheduled nature trips, you may wish to make it a family outing, or you may just want to get "away from it all" and go by yourself.

The equipment you carry will depend on your specific interests, how much hiking or driving you plan to do, and how long you plan to stay out.

There are a number of rules, some dictated by common sense and others by law, that should be observed on any field trip. They are:

1. Do not pick flowers or remove plants from alongside highways.

2. Do not collect plants or animals in state parks.

3. Do not throw litter from your car window.

4. Always obtain permission before entering private property. If collecting of specimens is planned, specific approval should be sought. When permission is granted, treat the landowner's property with respect. Do not damage fences, trample agricultural crops, help yourself to fruit or vegetables, annoy livestock, or leave the messy remains of your lunch behind.

5. If you have overturned logs and rocks or dug holes in the ground in your search for specimens, always replace things just as you found them so that the animal communities using those particular habitats will be disturbed as little as possible.

6. Regardless of what nature object you may collect, never take more than you have a legitimate use

for; and if a rare species is involved, restrain your collecting instinct and be satisfied to inspect specimens in a museum.

7. Always take a first-aid kit along and learn enough first aid from a scout handbook or Red Cross manual to take care of emergencies, including rattlesnake and Black Widow spider bites.

8. Do not hike into unfamiliar, uninhabited areas until you have studied a topographic map of the terrain, and then be sure to carry the map with you. Do not venture far into the back country alone.

9. Always tell someone at home or in camp just where you plan to go on your outing.

10. Be careful with matches, cigarettes, and fires. Always be sure your campfires or cookfires are completely out before you leave your campsite.

Try to keep these rules in mind as you set out to explore the bay region. For additional information on woodcraft and outdoor safety, see Harold Gatty's *Nature is Your Guide* (New York: Dutton, 1958), Mary V. Hood's *Nature and the Camper* (Los Angeles: Ward Ritchie, 1966) and Bradford Angier's *How to Stay Alive in the Woods* (New York: Collier, 1962).

Some of the outstanding field trips long favored by bay region naturalists are described here.

DESTINATION	LOCATION AND ROUTE
1. Moss Beach	Coastal San Mateo County; on State Hwy. 1, 7 miles north of Half Moon Bay.
2. Stinson Beach	Marin Coast; State Hwy. 1 just west of Mt. Tamalpais.
3. Drake's Bay	Marin Coast; turn west from Hwy. 1 just south of Point Reyes Station, follow Sir Francis Drake Blvd. to Drake's Bay.
4. Alum Rock Park	Foothills of Mt. Hamilton Range at end of Alum Rock Ave. east of San Jose.
5. Mount Hamilton	East of San Jose 21 miles on Mt. Hamilton Rd. Adventurous drivers may return via San Antonio Rd. on dirt roads and circle back through Patterson or Livermore.
6. Mount Diablo	In central Contra Costa County; may be approached by Green Valley Rd. from Alamo or Danville or by Ignacio Valley Rd. and Mt. Diablo Blvd. from Walnut Creek.
7. Mount St. Helena	At juncture of Napa, Lake, and Sonoma counties just west of State Hwy. 29 between Calistoga and Middletown.
8. Mount Tamalpais	Marin County just west of Mill Valley; approached by Bolinas—Fairfax Rd. and Ridgecrest Blvd. from the north and Muir Woods Rd. or Panoramic Hwy. from south.

NATURE FEATURES	COMMENTS
Marine and shore life; tide pools especially good at low tide; consult tide tables in newspaper for best dates and times.	Rocky beach; favorite study area for marine biology students.
Marine and shore life; also Monarch Butterflies sometimes overwinter on "butterfly" trees near here.	Sandy beach; a state park with camping and picnicking facilities.
Marine and shore life; good "beachcombing" after a storm.	Sandy beach; coastal prairie grasslands along road across peninsula.
Excellent for birds, insects, reptiles, amphibians, mammals, plants.	A wooded canyon; traditional study area for San Jose State College natural history classes.
Good for birds, insects, mammals, wild flowers, trees, stars; Lick Observatory is open to public Friday evenings; write for reservation.	Highest point in the Diablo Range—4,209 feet.
Birds, insects, plants, reptiles, amphibians, mammals; remarkable view of bay region and Great Central Valley on a clear day.	State park with camping and picnicking facilities.
Birds, insects, plants, mammals, reptiles, amphibians.	Highest point in the bay region—4,344 feet.
Birds, insects, plants, mammals, reptiles, amphibians.	State park with camping and picnicking facilities.

DESTINATION	LOCATION AND ROUTE
9. Big Basin Redwoods State Park	West of State Hwy. 9 in Santa Cruz Mountains north of Boulder Creek.
10. San Mateo County Memorial Park	On Pescadero Creek between Pescadero and La Honda; may be approached from Coast Hwy. (State Route 1) or Skyline Blvd. (State Route 5).
11. Corral Hollow	Extreme eastern edge of Alameda County; take Tesla Rd. southeast from Livermore or Corral Hollow Rd. south from Tracy Expressway just before reaching Tracy.
12. Searsville Lake—Jasper Ridge	In hills back of Palo Alto, at juncture of Portola Rd. and Sand Hill Rd.; approach from Woodside or Menlo Park. Obtain permission to enter Jasper Ridge from Director, Natural History Museum, Stanford Campus.
13. Mount Madonna	Just north of Hecker Pass (State Route 152) between Gilroy and Watsonville.
14. Stevens Creek	West of San Jose in foothills of Santa Cruz Mts.; follow Stevens Creek Rd. through Cupertino and Monte Vista, turn south just before reaching Kaiser Aluminum Plant.
15. East Bay Regional Parks	In Berkeley Hills from in back of El Cerrito to above San Leandro; many approaches.
16. Bay Farm Island (Also margins of bay in many places)	Take Hegenberger Rd. off Eastshore Freeway, or Otis Dr. from Alameda. Drive around bay on roads near the water.
17. Lake Merritt	In downtown Oakland.
18. Stow Lake	In Golden Gate Park, San Francisco.

NATURE FEATURES	COMMENTS
Redwood forest, birds, insects, deer, reptiles, amphibians.	State park with camping and picnicking facilities.
Redwood forest, birds, insects, mammals, reptiles, amphibians.	County park with camping and picnicking facilities.
Semidesert fauna and flora; snakes, lizards, insects.	Intermittent stream in a canyon that is essentially an arm of the Great Central Valley floor.
Birds, insects, plants, reptiles, amphibians.	Private park by lake with picnicking for a fee; Jasper Ridge, behind lake, is natural history preserve of Stanford University.
Birds, insects, plants.	A Santa Clara County park with camping and picnicking facilities.
Birds, insects, plants, reptiles, amphibians; very good for aquatic insects.	A Santa Clara County park with camping and picnicking facilities.
Variety of plant and animal life; museums and nature trails.	Barbecue pits, picnicking, recreational facilities, organized nature program.
Shore birds, also ducks and other water birds, particularly during migration.	Bay, mud flats at low tide, and salt marshes.
Many ducks, particularly in winter.	Lake formed from dredged salt marsh connected to bay.
Many ducks, particularly in winter.	Artificial fresh-water lake. Organized nature program.

WHERE TO OBTAIN HELP

There are many institutions and organizations that can provide assistance in learning about nature.

Audubon Nature Training sessions operated by the Golden Gate Audubon Society, in cooperation with Berkeley's Adult School and Department of Parks and Recreation, provide adult leaders of youth with outdoor education in an urban environment. Schedules on "How To Explore Nature in the City" may be obtained from Audubon Nature Training, 1749 Grove St., Berkeley, Calif. 94709 (549-1038).

Local Audubon Branches and Affiliates.—There are six active Branches and one Affiliate in the Bay Region who have regular schedules of meetings and field trips as announced in their monthly Bulletins. Information can be obtained from National Audubon Society, Bay Area Educational Services, 1749A Grove St., Berkeley, Calif. 94709 (849-1980).

Richardson Bay Wildlife Sanctuary and Education Center provides programs in cooperation with schools and groups. 376 Greenwood Beach Rd., Tiburon, Calif. 94920 (388-2424).

Audubon Canyon Ranch is a wildlife sanctuary and education center. Open to the public weekends and holidays. Group visits by appointment. Shoreline Hwy. Rt. 1, Stinson Beach, Calif. 94970 (868-0563).

The Oakland Museum.—A museum of California and the west. For information write Natural Science Division, 1000 Oak St., Oakland, Calif. 94607.

Cooper Ornithological Society.—Meets first Thursday

of month, from October to May, in Room 2503, Life Sciences Building, University of California, Berkeley.

Northern California Malacozoölogical Club.—Meets from 8 to 10 P.M. on the first Tuesday of every month (except December), in Room 4005, Life Sciences Building (Department of Zoölogy), University of California, Berkeley. This club offers help to both beginning and advanced students of mollusks.

California Academy of Sciences, Golden Gate Park, San Francisco.—Offers a wide variety of nature and science activities for Californians of all ages. Principal exhibits open to the public include Steinhart Aquarium, Simson African Hall (containing mounted mammals from Africa in natural settings), North American Hall (a general natural history museum), Morrison Planetarium, and a museum of photography. Scientific collections of western plants, animals, rocks, minerals, and fossils are also maintained for the use of qualified students and research specialists.

The California Academy of Sciences holds a monthly meeting that is open to the public, as are the regular meetings of the Astronomy Section and the Student Section. Other organizations that also meet at the Academy are the San Francisco Aquarium Society, California Horticultural Society, California Botanical Club, Pacific Coast Entomological Society, and the San Francisco Zoölogical Society.

Information on membership, meetings, public lectures held at the Academy, and natural history publications of the Academy may be obtained by writing to California Academy of Sciences, Golden Gate Park, San Francisco, California 94118.

The Sierra Club.—Best described by this statement from the *Sierra Club Bulletin:* ". . . founded in 1892, . . . devoted . . . to the study and protection of national scenic resources, particularly those of mountain regions. Participation is invited in the program to enjoy and preserve wilderness, wildlife, forests, and streams." This is the West's leading organization devoted to full enjoyment of the out-of-doors and conservation of natural resources. For information on activities of this organization, write to Sierra Club, 1050 Mills Tower, San Francisco, California 94104.

Junior Museums.—A well-rounded program of nature study is offered for young naturalists in the bay region. Exhibits, small zoos, aquaria, terraria, arts and crafts, field trips, films, talks, and animal-lending "libraries" are among the features available at the eleven Junior Museums now operating in this area. These museums are: Alexander Lindsay Junior Museum (Walnut Creek), Hayward Art and Science Center (Hayward), Josephine D. Randall Junior Museum (San Francisco), Junior Center of Art and Science (Oakland), Junior Field Museum (Berkeley), Louise A. Boyd Natural Science Museum (San Rafael), Palo Alto Junior Museum (Palo Alto), Rotary Natural Science Center (Oakland), San Mateo County Junior Museum (San Mateo), Junior Academy of the California Academy of Sciences (San Francisco), and Youth Science Institute (San Jose). Specific information on the programs and locations of the various museums may be obtained from Bay Area Junior Museum Directors Association, 1901 First Ave., Walnut Creek, Calif. 94596.

Audubon Junior Program. Many youth groups are already active in the bay region. To find out if there is a group near your home write to National Audubon Society, Bay Area Educational Services, 1749A Grove St., Berkeley, Calif. 94709.

Other Organizations.—Your community may also have a rock and mineral society, a malacological society, botanical society, or other science club. Check with your local Chamber of Commerce, college science department, or high school science teacher for information on other nature organizations.

Publications.—Magazines and bulletins are an important source of news and information about nature, naturalists, and nature books:

1. *Pacific Discovery*—a bimonthly periodical devoted to popular natural history of the West. Published by the California Academy of Sciences.

2. *Sunset*—a general monthly magazine devoted primarily to travel, home, and garden in the West, but also contains many articles on nature. Published by Lane Publishing Company, Menlo Park, California.

3. Printed or mimeographed monthly bulletins are available from most of the Audubon Society Chapters and Affiliates.

4. Three national magazines that are outstanding in the popular natural history field and that carry many articles of interest to bay region residents are: *Natural History* (Central Park W., N.Y., N.Y. 10024), *Audubon* (1130 Fifth Ave., N.Y., N.Y. 10028), and *National Wildlife* (1412 16 St., N.W., Washington, D.C. 20036).

5. Other useful magazines include *American Forests* (American Forestry Association, 919 17th St. N.W., Washington, D.C. 20006), *Aquarium Journal* (San Francisco Aquarium Society, Steinhart Aquarium, Golden Gate Park, San Francisco, Ca. 94118), *Sky and Telescope* (Harvard College Observatory, 60 Garden St., Cambridge, Mass. 02138), and *Gems and Minerals* (P. O. Box 687, Mentown, Ca. 92359).

6. Miscellaneous publications of value in learning about nature include *Audubon Nature Bulletins and Charts* (National Audubon Society) 70 bulletins and 15 charts available, and *Cornell Rural School Leaflets* (Cornell University, Ithaca, New York) many back issues available.

Radio and Television.—Several radio and television stations present interesting nature and science programs regularly or from time to time. For dates and times of programs, see published schedules or write to your local stations or to the radio and television columnists of your local newspaper.

Supplies and Equipment.—Listed below are a few of the places where supplies and equipment for nature study can be obtained:

1. Clo Wind, 827 Congress Ave., Pacific Grove, Ca. 93950.
2. Wards of California, P. O. Box 1749, Monterey, Ca. 93942.
3. General Biological Supply House, Inc., 8200 South Hoyne Ave., Chicago, Ill.
4. Scientific Supplies Co., 600 Spokane St., Seattle, Wash. 98104.
5. Bio Metal, P. O. Box 61, Santa Monica, Ca. 90401.

SUGGESTED REFERENCES

GENERAL

Drimmer, Frederick (ed.). *The Animal Kingdom.* 3 vols. New York: Greystone Press, 1954.

Palmer, E. Laurence. *Field Book of Natural History.* New York: McGraw-Hill, 1949.

Simpson, George G., Colin S. Pittendrigh, and Lewis H. Tiffany. *Life: An Introduction to Biology.* New York: Harcourt, Brace, 1957.

IDENTIFICATION GUIDES AND MANUALS

Hoffman, Ralph. *Birds of the Pacific States.* Boston: Houghton Mifflin, 1927.

Peterson, Roger T. *A Field Guide to Western Birds.* Boston: Houghton Mifflin, rev. 1961.

Berry, William D., Elizabeth Berry, *Mammals of the San Francisco Bay Region.* Berkeley: University of California Press, 1959.

Burt, William H., and Richard P. Grossenheider. *A Field Guide to the Mammals.* Boston: Houghton Mifflin, rev. 1965.

Ingles, Lloyd G. *Mammals of the Pacific States.* Stanford: Stanford University Press, 1965.

Murie, Olaus. *A Field Guide to Animal Tracks.* Boston: Houghton Mifflin, 1954.

Stebbins, Robert C. *Amphibians and Reptiles of Western North America.* New York: McGraw-Hill, 1954.

Stebbins, Robert C. *Reptiles and Amphibians of the San Francisco Bay Region.* Berkeley: University of California Press, 1959.

Stebbins, Robert C. *Field Guide to Western Reptiles and Amphibians.* Boston: Houghton Mifflin, 1966.

Swain, Ralph B. *Insect Guide*. New York: Doubleday, 1948.

Usinger, Robert L. *Aquatic Insects of California.* Berkeley: University of California Press, 1956.

Abbott, R. Tucker. *American Seashells.* New York: Van Nostrand, 1954.

Morris, Percy A. *A Field Guide to Shells of the Pacific Coast and Hawaii, including Shells of the Gulf of California.* Boston: Houghton Mifflin, 1966.

Ricketts, Edward F., and Jack Calvin. Revised by Joel W. Hedgpeth. *Between Pacific Tides.* Stanford: Stanford University Press, 1952.

Comstock, John H. *The Spider Book.* Ithaca: Comstock Publishing Co., 1948.

Gertsch, Willis J. *American Spiders.* Princeton: Van Nostrand, 1949.

Jepson, Willis L. *A Manual of the Flowering Plants of California.* Berkeley: University of California Press, 1957.

Metcalf, Woodbridge W. *Native Trees of the San Francisco Bay Region.* Berkeley: University of California Press, 1959.

Armstrong, Margaret. *Field Book of Western Wildflowers.* New York: Putnam, 1912.

McMinn, Howard E. *An Illustrated Manual of California Shrubs.* Berkeley: University of California Press, 1964.

Parsons, Mary Elizabeth, *The Wild Flowers of California.* (ed. Roxana S. Ferris) New York: Dover, 1966.

Pough, Frederick H. *A Field Guide to the Rocks and Minerals.* Boston: Houghton Mifflin, 1953.